MICHELE ARN

JOURNAL

LIGHT FOR MY PATH

A BIBLE STUDY

STYLE

MAGAZINE

IN HIS GRACE MINISTRIES LLC

ISBN-13: 978-1-7351373-0-8

Published by In His Grace Ministries LLC

Book website: https://www.inhisgrace.com/product/journal-light-for-my-path/

Dedication

To Risa, it has been a pleasure and my joy to watch you grow into a beautiful young lady. You are a force to be reckoned with, someone who is strong and someone who can have a significant influence in the lives of others. God is going to do great things through you if you allow Him to do so. I hope you will find out who you are within these pages. God is so good, and He is so in love with you. Press into Him daily. Get to know who He is and what His promises are. Soak in every aspect of God and His Word. Hide His Word deep within who you are, because from His Word, you will grow into who He created you to be.
With Love

HOW TO USE:

Devotional day: Read the Bible verse. Pray over the verse and your day. Read the text. Study the verse. Meditate, filling your mind with God's truth and His Words. What does it mean to you? You will see beside a few words and phrases an asterisk * this will mean that there is a definition in the dictionary. See dictionary explanation below.

Memory verse: Each day will have the same Bible verse at the bottom of the pray about everything page. Read and re-read this verse and memorize it and keep it close to your heart.

Dictionary: Is found in the back of the magazine on page 109-110. Here you will find words and phrases from the devotionals with their meaning to gain better clarity and understanding of their intention and meaning.

Questions: There are two questions asked in this space from the day's devotion. Think about them for a while before you respond. There is space below for your answers. Answer honestly, with vulnerability to the Lord. Because He already knows what you are thinking and how you are feeling. Be open and honest with Him.

Keywords: This is a place for you to write out any words that might have stuck out to you from the day's devotional.

My thoughts: You can use this space to write what you felt when you read the devotional, or to expand on your keywords.

Pray about everything: Prayer requests and praise reports

Creative space: I intend this space for you to use in any way you feel led. Draw, write, prayers. Anything you are feeling in the moment.

89

35

Contents

51

7

Wisdom

If you need *Wisdom*,

ask our generous God, and He will give it to you. He will not rebuke you for asking.

James 1:5 NLT

"If you need wisdom, ask our generous God, and He
will give it to you. He will not rebuke you for asking."

James 1:5 NLT

A situation comes along, a decision needs to be made, but you lack understanding. You are uncertain about how to proceed. The best thing to do is to stop for a moment or two and pray. Talk with God, not just to Him, but have an actual conversation with Him about what is going on. James tells us that if we lack wisdom then we should ask God for some. God won't judge you for not knowing the answer. But He will delight in you asking for help. So much so He will give you wisdom when asked, generously, and without fault.

The world's wisdom and God's wisdom are different. So make sure that when you ask for wisdom, you understand exactly what you are asking for. With God's wisdom comes responsibility in how you use it. The world says that having wisdom is about experience, about following after the things you want. Looking to one's self instead of looking to God. God's wisdom James says in 3:17 NLT, is pure. Peace-loving, gentle, all the time. Full of mercy and is sincere. *"But the wisdom from above is first of all pure. It is also peace-loving, gentle at all times, and willing to yield to others. It is full of mercy and the fruit of good deeds. It shows no favoritism and is always sincere."*

So when you ask for wisdom, ask in faith, without doubt, that God will provide and take care of your needs. When you pray and talk with God don't forget to listen. Listen to the Words of the Holy Spirit, pause for a moment to hear God's prompting. In faith, pursue, move forward. In faith, with wisdom given, God will guide you to what you should do or where you should go.

Questions

How should you ask for wisdom?

How does God provide for your needs?

Date:

Key words:

My Thoughts

Pray about everything

Don't worry about anything; instead, pray about everything.
Tell God what you need, and thank Him for all He has done.
Philippians 4:6 NLT

Guidance

YOur WOrD is A LAMP to GUiDE MY fEEt AND A LIGHt for MY PAtH.

PsALm 119:105 nLt

"Your word is
a lamp to
guide my feet
and a light
for my path."

Psalm 119:105 NLT

You might have heard it said that God's Word is the light to your path. But what does this mean? God has laid out for you how you are to act and react. How you are to live out your life. This world might seem dark at times, but God floods the earth with His power and greatness. Just look around at what He has created. The beauty of it all. God's Word is the lamp to our feet and the light to our path. God with His Word, the Bible, tells us how as *Jesus followers we are to be. We are to show up differently than those who don't believe. God has called you to a greater purpose. Seek after God and His Word and He will guide you to where you need to go and what you need to do. In the Bible, it is clearly stated how a Jesus follower should behave. How are you to live as a Jesus follower? How are you to live out your *calling? Here are just a few examples of how to live your life as a Jesus follower. You are to trust in God at all times; Psalm 62:8. You are to not let any unwholesome talk come out of your mouths; Ephesians 4:29. You are to not be quickly angered; James 1:20, Proverbs 16:32. Do not judge others; Matthew 7:1-2. Work hard in everything you do; Colossians 3:23. Be honest; Proverbs 12:22. Do not use the Lord's name in vain; Exodus 20:7. You are God's *workmanship created to do good works; Ephesians 2:10. Be doers of the Word; James 1:22. Be gentle and self-controlled; Galatians 5:22-23. Be selfless, and care for others; Philippians 2:4. Share the gospel; Psalm 96:3. Be imitators of God; Ephesians 5:1. Love the Lord you God with all your heart, mind, and soul, love your neighbor as yourself; Luke 10:27.

You are a light to the world; shine bright. Don't allow your light to be dimmed. Love God and follow closely after Him.

9

Questions

Find other Bible verses on how you are to live as a Jesus follower.

Now, what do these mean to you?

Date:

Key words

My Thoughts

Pray about everything

Don't worry about anything; instead, pray about everything.
Tell God what you need, and thank Him for all He has done.
Philippians 4:6 NLT

Compassion

BE KIND AND
COMPASSIONATE
TO ONE
ANOTHER,
FORGIVING
EACH OTHER,
JUST AS IN
CHRIST GOD
FORGAVE YOU.

Ephesians 4:32 NIV

"BE KIND AND COMPASSIONATE TO ONE ANOTHER, FORGIVING EACH OTHER, JUST AS IN CHRIST GOD FORGAVE YOU."

EPHESIANS 4:32 NIV

How many times have you heard it said to be kind to one another? Have *compassion towards others. Forgive others for the things they have done or said to you. But what is it truly to be kind and compassionate to someone else? And let's not forget that we are even supposed to be kind to our enemies. You are even to be kind to those that you might not like very much. And we are to forgive even those people who don't ask for forgiveness. Now, this does not make what that person did all right. This does not give anyone the right to use you or to insult or hurt you. This does however present a situation where you can rise above the hurt feelings and the upset that you might have towards someone for what they did and turn it into something good. Let me explain. If someone calls you a name how would you respond? Would you call them a name right back? It can be very tempting to do so, but God calls for us to do something different. We are to be kind instead of mean. We are to show them the love of Christ. Think about this for a second, you might just be the first person to ever show them who Christ is. And what an honor that would be. If they are already a follower of Jesus, remember that we all fall short of the glory of God, and can make mistakes from time to time. Be kind in your response. Be compassionate towards them as they might be going through something you know nothing about. *"Be happy with those who are happy, and *weep with those who weep."* Romans 12:15 NLT. Then you forgive. *Forgiveness is powerful. Forgiveness has the power to set you free, or it has the power to hold you captive. If you forgive others, you release them and yourself and allow God to do a work in their heart and their lives. If you choose not to forgive you end up holding onto the hurt and it sits there like a rock heavy on your heart. And sometimes it can be too much to carry on your own. God calls us to forgive. The Bible even says that if we do not forgive that, God will not forgive you for your sins. *"But if you refuse to forgive others, your Father will not forgive your sins."* Matthew 6:15 NLT. Within forgiveness, you have compassion, *kindness and love. Look to Jesus, He will guide you, He will help you release any hurt that might still be there.

Kindness and compassion go beyond when someone does something wrong. When you allow Jesus to walk beside you, being kind and compassionate will come more naturally to you.

Questions

Has there ever been a time when you were not kind? Explain
Have you asked God for forgiveness?

How can you show others kindness and compassion?

Date:

Key words:

My Thoughts

Pray about everything

Don't worry about anything; instead, pray about everything.
Tell God what you need, and thank Him for all He has done.
Philippians 4:6 NLT

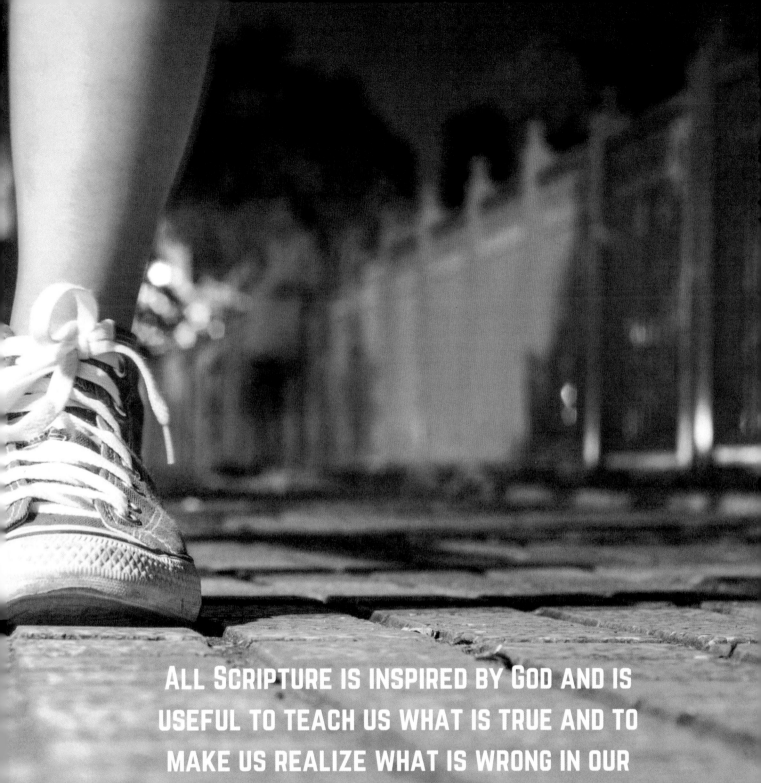

All Scripture is inspired by God and is useful to teach us what is true and to make us realize what is wrong in our lives. It corrects us when we are wrong and teaches us to do what is right.

2 timothy 3:16 NLT

creative
space

Confident

Don't let anyone look down on you because you are

but set an example for the believers in speech, in conduct, in love, in faith and in purity.

1 Timothy 4:12 NIV

Don't you just hate it when someone says that you can't do something because you are too young? Well, I hate to break the news to you, but sometimes you are just too young to do or say or wear certain things. But with God, with His Word, you are never too young. God *made you on purpose for a purpose. Although, here Paul was speaking to Timothy about his leadership within the church, but you can claim this as your own. Place on yourself God's Words. Internalize them so you can pull from them when needed. Paul is saying to not let anyone look down on you because you are young. You are an important part of this world. Needed and loved. But within not letting others look down on you because of your age, Paul says that you need to set an example for other believers. And even those who don't believe. Be an example in how you talk, in how you behave, how you love, your *faith, and in your purity. But how you might ask? By learning about who God is. By studying His Word, the Bible. Learn what the Bible says, memorize what the Bible says. Then walk in faith, walk in love, and walk in the *Scriptures.

"Don't let anyone look down on you because you are young, but set an example for the believers in speech, in conduct, in love, in faith and in purity."

1 Timothy 4:12 NIV

Questions

How can you set an example for others?

How do you walk in faith, love, and the Scriptures?

Date:

Key words:

My Thoughts

Pray about everything

Don't worry about anything; instead, pray about everything.
Tell God what you need, and thank Him for all He has done.
Philippians 4:6 NLT

Honor

Children, obey your parents in everything, for this pleases the Lord.

Colossians 3:20 NIV

For this pleases the Lord. *Honoring and *obeying your parents is your job right now. This is your responsibility as their child. The *Scriptures are clear on how you are to act and react. Ephesians 6:2-3 NIV says; *"Honor your father and mother"—which is the first commandment with a promise—" so that it may go well with you and that you may enjoy long life on the earth."* In honoring and obeying your parents, it is their responsibility to teach, instruct, and to train you up to be a woman of God. To teach you the Scriptures and how to follow in Jesus' footsteps. As your parents, they are to do this lovingly and gently, not in a way that will cause you to become discouraged or frustrated. They are to *lead you to the cross. Just remember as your parents they are not to ask or require you to do anything that goes against the Lord and His teachings. However, remember to give your parents *grace when they make mistakes, because just like you they are not perfect. And you can still honor someone even if their actions are not worth honoring, it's who they are that counts. And Jesus extends us all grace, so we should in turn extend grace to others.

"Children, obey your parents in everything, for this pleases the Lord"

Colossians 3:20 NIV

Questions

How do you honor and obey your parents?

What does lead you to the cross mean to you?

Date:

Key words:

My Thoughts

33

Pray about everything

Don't worry about anything; instead, pray about everything.
Tell God what you need, and thank Him for all He has done.
Philippians 4:6 NLT

34

God's Word

I have hidden

YOUR WORD

~

in my heart that I might not sin *against You*

Psalm 119:11 NLT

Knowing the *Scriptures is so important in your walk with God. Knowing the Scriptures is a way to get to know who God is and a way to find out who you are in Him. Just like any other relationship, it takes time together to learn about one another and it takes this time to grow. *Intentionally placing God's Word inside your heart is an act of *worship to the Lord.

Knowing God's truths, holding onto them, and hiding them in your heart will create in you a well to draw from. *A well when filled will never run dry. Meaning the Holy Spirit whom Jesus gave to us as a gift the moment we believed, courses through us like a river. The Holy Spirit, that Jesus gives, will flow through you and will create in you a well to draw from. In good times and in bad. If you continue to draw from God's Word through the Holy Spirit your well will not dry up. It will spring forth your faith in Him, it will spring forth your hope in Him. It will spring forth your eternal life in Him. When needed you can draw from this well. God's Word when known, will help to keep you from sinning. Because you know what is right and what is wrong in God's eyes. And you want nothing more than to please Him.

Piece by piece, word by word, read, learn, and store the Scriptures in the depths of your heart. Meditate, filling your mind with God's Word every single day.

"I HAVE HIDDEN YOUR WORD IN MY HEART, THAT I MIGHT NOT SIN AGAINST YOU"

Psalm 119:11 NLT

Questions

Why is it important to be in God's Word every day?

What can you do to make sure you stay in God's Word every day?

Date:

Key words:

My Thoughts

Pray about everything

Don't worry about anything; instead, pray about everything.
Tell God what you need, and thank Him for all He has done.
Philippians 4:6 NLT

I have hidden your word
in my heart, that I might
not sin against you.

Psalm 119:11 NLT

Creative Space

Blessed

BLESSED IS THE ONE
WHOSE SIN THE

Lord

WILL NEVER COUNT
AGAINST THEM

ROMANS 4:8 NIV

How amazing is God's love for us? To learn and understand that He chose you. He made you with His very own hands. Molded and shaped you into who He needed you to be.

Through Jesus, we are saved. Because of Jesus' selfless act for you and me, all of our sins have been forgiven. Jesus went to the cross, endured an enormous amount of pain to take on all of our sins. When you sin, and you will, it will not be counted against you. Yes, there can be earthly consequences for your sin, but eternally Jesus will stand up and defend you, He will once again stand in your place and take on your sins. However, when you sin you will need to make things right. Not only with God, but with the other person and with yourself.

There is a process in doing this. Confess, repent, and restore.

Confess what you did to those who need to know. Admit your mistakes to them, to yourself, and to God. Repent, turn from your sin and your mistakes and turn to Jesus instead. Restore, repair the situation, the relationship if possible between you and the other person. Restore your relationship with the Lord.

In doing these things you will find peace. Turning to Jesus, you will find yourself. In your relationship with Jesus, your sins will be forgiven. You are then *blessed within, sins covered for all time.

Questions

Do you have any sins you haven't confessed to God?

What is the process of repairing relationships?

Date:

Key words:

My Thoughts

Pray about everything

Don't worry about anything; instead, pray about everything.
Tell God what you need, and thank Him for all He has done.
Philippians 4:6 NLT

Friendship

THE *heartfelt*

COUNSEL OF A
FRIEND IS AS

sweet

AS PERFUME AND
INCENSE

PROVERBS 27:9 NLT

"The heartfelt counsel of a friend is as sweet as perfume and incense" Proverbs 27:9 NLT

Friendships are so very important in life. When you surround yourself with the right people, your walk with the Lord should grow. The people you choose to be around can change the course of your life. They can influence you in good or bad ways. You have to be able to know who is right for you and who is not. Perhaps make a checklist on how you choose a friend. For example: Are they believers? Do they listen to and obey their parents? Are they kind in word and actions?

1 Corinthians 15:33 NLT says; *"Don't be fooled by those who say such things, for "bad company *corrupts good character."* If they are willing to disobey or do something that they know they should not do, walk away. It is all right for you to end a friendship when the other person is not acting like they should. Proverbs 1:15 says to stay far away from people who are willing to do wrong. It is *wisdom and *discernment that will help you identify who you should have as a friend.

Find someone who believes in the Lord. Someone who can walk beside you on your journey in getting to know the Lord. Find a friend who will pray with you and for you. Find someone who will challenge you in growing in the *Scriptures. Find a friend who will challenge you to be a better version of yourself. Someone who will love you despite your awkward quirks, or your mistakes. Find a friend who you can cry with, someone you can pour your heart out to, and know that they will keep your confidence. Someone you can trust. Someone who will give you Godly words when you need it most. A friend who you can laugh with, even when they or you make a silly mistake.

When you find this friend, accept them for who they are and love them. Pray for them and treasure them, and treat them as the gift that they are direct from the Lord.

Questions

What should you look for in a friend?

How do you maintain a Godly friendship?

Date:

Key words

My Thoughts

Pray about everything

Don't worry about anything; instead, pray about everything.
Tell God what you need, and thank Him for all He has done.
Philippians 4:6 NLT

Purity

PSALM 119:9 NLT

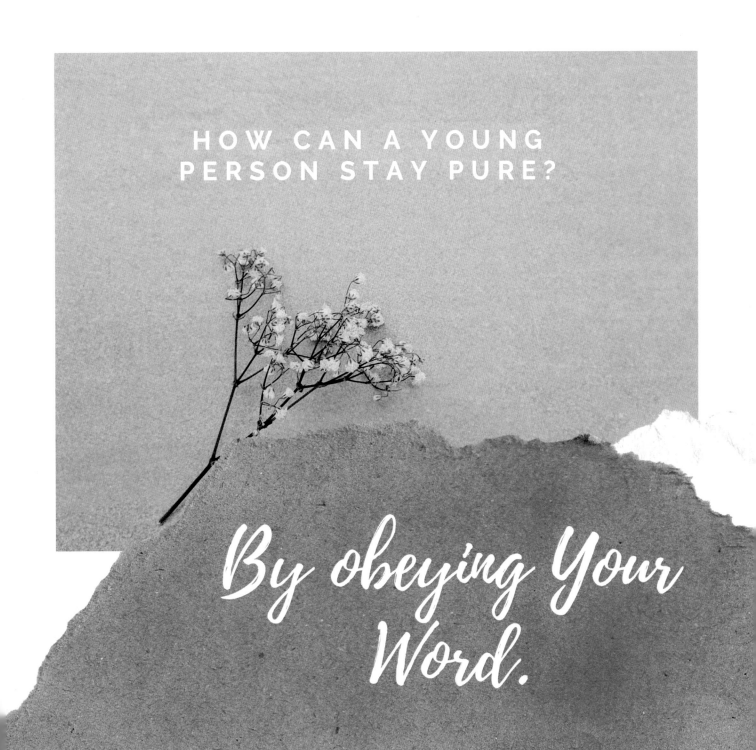

HOW CAN A YOUNG PERSON STAY PURE?

By obeying Your Word.

"How can a young person stay pure?
By obeying Your word."

Psalm 119:9 NLT

The quest for purity is so difficult, especially right now. With the rise of social media and the internet, to the beliefs of some of those around you. Right now more than ever you need to protect yourself from the attacks that the enemy is throwing towards you. Stand firm, stay strong, and know that your purity is something to be treasured. Psalm 119:9 NLT addresses this with a question, and the answer. *"How can a young person stay pure? By obeying Your Word"* This is another reason why knowing God's Word is so important. When you know His Word you are equipped and you are armed with the *confidence to stay the course. What you allow to enter into your life will affect your life. Make sure that who you hang out with, what you read, what you listen to, and what you watch do not lend to *temptation. You are to put aside earthly desires. Romans 13:14 NIV says; *"Rather, clothe yourselves with the Lord Jesus Christ, and do not think about how to gratify the desires of the flesh."*

The Bible is filled with verses speaking to your purity. How you are to act and react. How you should conduct yourself daily. Purity encompasses so much, how you talk, how you dress, how you act, what your thought life is like, how you act in private, and with others. When you cling to your purity, God will bless you. *"God blesses those whose hearts are pure, for they will see God."* Matthew 5:8 NLT.

Remember that knowing God's Word will help you stay pure. Let His Word soak into every inch of your body, mind, and soul. With Him, you will be able to stand against the enemy.

"Do you not know that your bodies are temples of the Holy Spirit, who is in you, whom you have received from God? You are not your own; you were bought at a price. Therefore honor God with your bodies." 1 Corinthians 6:19-20 NIV.

Questions

What other Bible verses speak about purity?

What can you do to protect your purity?

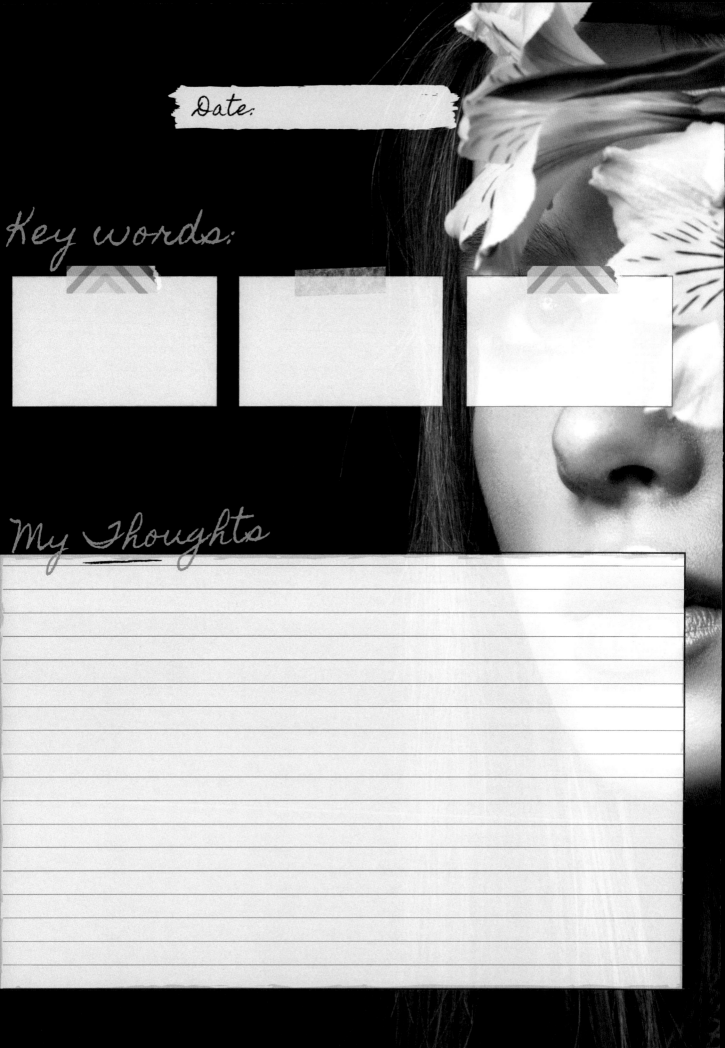

Date:

Key words:

My Thoughts

Pray about everything

Don't worry about anything; instead, pray about everything.
Tell God what you need, and thank Him for all He has done.
Philippians 4:6 NLT

YOU LIGHT A LAMP for ME.
THE LORD, MY GOD,
LIGHTS UP MY DARKNESS.

PSALM 18:28 NLT

Pray

REJOICE
ALWAYS
PRAY
CONTINUALLY

1 THESSALONIANS 5:16-17 NIV

Your life might not always be rainbows and sunshine. Regret, heartache, upset, and frustrations might enter the picture. But God, God says that we should *rejoice always and *pray continually. I don't think God wants us to live a life of waiting. Waiting for the heartache and pain to go away before we are happy and rejoice. Waiting for the upset and frustrations to go away before we pray. I believe that it is just the opposite. That despite these things, God calls us to rejoice in our sufferings. Because our sufferings prove our faith. Our sufferings refine us into who God needs us to be to fulfill the *calling He has on our lives. To truly rely on God, we need to have reasons to. We can't understand what it means to trust in Him if we never experience failure, heartache, frustrations, or pain. Through these, we are being *refined by fire. All of our impurities burned away. In this process, we learn to rejoice. We learn to pray always. There might be times when life is hard, but you have this sense of peace, this joy that you know cannot be of this world. It is deep within you, touching your heart and soul. Your gut just knows that this is not of you, but God. There is no other explanation as to where your peace and joy come from. God is your source of joy. He is your source of peace. Pray continually, in doing so you will hear the Words of the Lord speak to you, and you will feel His presence all around. The result will be joy, pure joy. Because you believe in Him, you trust in Him, and you praise Him with everything that you have.

"Don't worry about anything; instead, pray about everything. Tell God what you need, and thank Him for all He has done." Philippians 4:6 NLT

"Rejoice always, pray continually,"

1 Thessalonians 5:16-17 NIV

Questions

How can you rejoice through the regret, heartache, upset and frustrations?

What does being refined by fire mean to you?

Date:

Key words:

My Thoughts

Pray about everything

Don't worry about anything; instead, pray about everything.
Tell God what you need, and thank Him for all He has done.
Philippians 4:6 NLT

Trust

TRUST IN THE LORD WITH ALL YOUR HEART; DO NOT DEPEND ON YOUR OWN UNDERSTANDING SEEK HIS WILL IN ALL YOU DO, AND HE WILL SHOW YOU WHICH PATH TO TAKE.

Proverbs 3:5-6 NLT

Just like placing God's Word on the *tablet of your heart, you also need to trust God with your whole heart. A trust so complete that it will not falter. We can sometimes get confused with a lack of understanding and thinking that our trust is wavering However, it's not that your trust or faith is lacking, it's your understanding of the situation that is lacking.

Sometimes when we are looking at this thing called life, we don't always see clearly what it is that we are to do or where we are to go. We pray with hope and *expectancy, and sometimes we *pray without ceasing. But our view and our perspective are limited. We do not see the entire picture. But God, He sees the entire picture. He knows what was, what is, and what will come. One day what God sees will become clear to us whether this side of heaven or after. Cling to His promises and lean into Him and His understanding in your situation. *"For I know the plans I have for you, declares the Lord, plans to prosper you and not harm you, plans to give you hope and a future"* Jeremiah 29:11 NIV.

When you trust with your entire heart and you give way for God to move in your life, He will show you the way. When you allow God access into your life, He will direct your steps. When all you desire is to do God's will He will delight in you. *"the Lord delights in those who fear him, who put their hope in his unfailing love."* Psalm 147:11 NIV.

Trust in the Lord with all your heart; do not depend on your own understanding. Seek His will in all you do, and He will show you which path to take."

Proverbs 3:5-6 NLT

Questions

How do you allow God access into your life?

How do you maintain your trust in God?

Date:

Key words:

My Thoughts

Pray about everything

Don't worry about anything; instead, pray about everything.
Tell God what you need, and thank Him for all He has done.
Philippians 4:6 NLT

Worship

Come, let us *Worship* and bow down. Let us *kneel* before the *Lord* our maker

PSALM 95:6 NLT

"Come, let us worship and bow down. Let us kneel before the Lord our maker"

Psalm 95:6 NLT

Come, Psalm 95:6 starts with, come with me, let us *worship and bow down together. Let us kneel together before the Lord. Whenever I hear the word come, I hear my grandbaby's voice "coming grammy, coming" She wants me to join her in whatever adventure she has in store at that moment. Come, her hand held out in anticipation that I will join her. When I take her by the hand and join her and teach her this is an expression of worship. And what sweet worship it is.

Often when worship is talked about people think only of singing, whether that be in church or listening to music on your own. This is true, but worship encompasses so much more than just music. Worship in its purest form is an act, an expression of honor and *reverence to the Lord. When you do something with awe and reverence for the Lord, this is worship.

We have the inner experience of worship, knowing, trusting, and loving God. And the outward expression of worship, the doing of things, acts of service, and acts of love.

Worship can look different to people and can show up in different ways. Let me explain. Yes, worship in our current culture and understanding is about singing, lifting our voices, and raising our arms to the Lord. And what an amazing and sweet encounter you can have with the Lord in doing so. But you can encounter and worship God in several ways. Worship can look like prayer, it can look like a sweet conversation with a trusted friend. We can express worship in helping someone in need. Worship can be done by connecting with the Lord through Bible study, and by getting to know His Word. The ability to and the way you can worship is endless.

So come, join me in worship and let's kneel before the Lord together.

Questions

In what ways can you express your worship?

In what ways can you have the inner experience of worship?

Date:

Key words:

My Thoughts

Pray about everything

Don't worry about anything; instead, pray about everything.
Tell God what you need, and thank Him for all He has done.
Philippians 4:6 NLT

84

Jesus spoke to the people once more and said, "I am the light of the world. If you follow me, you won't have to walk in darkness, because you will have the light that leads to life."

John 8:12 NLT

Creative space

Hope

May the God of hope fill you with all joy and peace as you trust in Him, so that you may

WITH HOPE

by the power of the Holy Spirit

Romans 15:13 NIV

"May the God of hope fill you with all joy and peace as you trust in Him, so that you may overflow with hope by the power of the Holy Spirit."

Romans 15:13 NIV

The hope of the world is so different from our hope in Christ. The hope of the world is wishing something would happen. Your fingers crossed, not knowing if what you are hoping for will happen. But hope in God is known, it is felt, it is a confident expectation in who God is and His promises for you.

The result of trusting in God is to be filled with joy and peace. From trust, joy, and peace you will overflow with hope. God is gracious and knows how to give good gifts to His children. The best gift one can get is knowing who Jesus is. Getting to know Him and His teachings. Growing ever closer to Him with each passing day.

Imagine overflowing with anything. Think about a tall glass of water. You take the time to fill the glass, each action, each step, it takes thought; it takes purpose. As you are holding the glass, you walk over to the sink, turn the knob, place the glass under the faucet, you watch as the glass is being filled. You keep filling the glass and before you know it; the water is pouring over the sides. Spilling over touching everything in its path. This is much like how getting to know Jesus is. When you are *intentional in reading God's Word. Studying what the Words on the page mean. Learning and memorizing the verses and what they mean and what they mean to you. You slowly at first are being filled, filled with purpose. Filled with the good news. Filled with the knowledge of God's promises to you. Filled with love, *grace, *forgiveness, and mercy. As the Words of God start flowing through you, God fills you with His joy and His peace, your trust in Him grows. And your faith and your hope begin to overflow. And as your hope continues to overflow, it touches those around you. You, even without knowing it, are making an impact in someone else's life.

Others will see your hope in the Lord. Your hope will be noticed. 1 Peter 3:15 NLT says; *"Instead, you must worship Christ as Lord of your life. And if someone asks about your hope as a believer, always be ready to explain it."*

Be prepared. Be ready. Overflow with hope.

Questions

What are some of God's promises to you?

_____
_____
_____
_____
_____
_____
_____
_____
_____
_____
_____
_____
_____
_____
_____
_____
_____
_____

Why do you hope and trust in the Lord?

_____
_____
_____
_____
_____
_____
_____
_____
_____
_____
_____
_____
_____

Date:

Key words:

My Thoughts

Pray about everything

Don't worry about anything; instead, pray about everything.
Tell God what you need, and thank Him for all He has done.
Philippians 4:6 NLT

Fruits of the Spirit

But the Holy Spirit produces this kind of fruit in our lives: love, joy, peace, patience, kindness, goodness, faithfulness, gentleness, and self-control. There is no law against these things!

- Galatians 5:22-23 NLT

They will know you by your fruit. How you act, what you say, how you present yourself. They will know whose you are. If you say that you are a *Jesus follower and you don't live by the *Scriptures, people will notice. And because you are a Jesus follower, people will hold you to a higher standard. Fair or not, this is how it goes. So do your best to live your life worthy of the name of Jesus.

Love will become greater, selfless. You will find different ways to express God's love. Joy is knowing and trusting Jesus. You can still *rejoice even when things are not going well. Because your gaze is looking out and upward. Not inward focusing on the problem at hand. Peace is being complete in God. Knowing that in a less than peaceful situation God is there. It is a wholeness when you know whose you are. Patience will grow, and you will be able to withstand the unknown, and the frustrations better. *Kindness to others, even if undeserved becomes easier and something you will want to express. Goodness will show up in your respect for others. In wanting to do the right thing. You will become gentle in your responses and your approach to things. Faithfulness to God and others will be something that will come naturally to you. Gentleness does not mean that you are weak. It means that you are humble in your words and your actions. Self-control gives you the ability to control your actions, your anger, and your responses to others. It gives you the ability to make the right choices in your life.

Your *faith in God is what others will see through the fruits of the Spirit. When you allow God to be Lord over your life, all of these things will find their rightful place. Meaning it will become easier for you to walk in the Spirit. Fulfilling and expressing love, joy, peace, patience, kindness, goodness, faithfulness, gentleness, and self-control.

"But the Holy Spirit produces this kind of fruit in our lives: love, joy, peace, patience, kindness, goodness, faithfulness, gentleness, and self-control. There is no law against these things!"

———

Galatians 5:22-23 NLT

Questions

Are you bearing fruit, or just have the appearance of bearing fruit?

How can you fulfill and express the fruits of the Spirit?

Date:

Key words:

My thoughts

Pray about everything

Don't worry about anything; instead, pray about everything.
Tell God what you need, and thank Him for all He has done.
Philippians 4:6 NLT

Goodwill

SO LET'S NOT GET TIRED OF

doing good.

AT JUST THE RIGHT TIME WE WILL REAP A HARVEST OF

blessing

IF WE DON'T GIVE UP.

"So let's not get tired of doing what is good. At just the right time we will reap a harvest of blessing if we don't give up."

Galatians 6:9 NLT

Doing the right thing can be hard. It can be tough sometimes to maintain your focus on God when there are so many *temptations and choices that pass you by daily. How should you respond when someone is mean? How do you respond when you are facing a choice to go along with the flow when others are not doing what they should be? Do you cave to peer pressure, or do you stand up for what is right? Do you argue with others, or do you try to keep the peace?

It can be tiresome at times, always doing the right thing. But sweet one, doing the right thing is what Jesus needs you to do. It allows others to see Jesus through you. It allows you to express who Jesus is through your actions, in your attitude, in how you talk. The list goes on. Jesus won't leave you without His gentle promptings in your life. The directions you should go. The choices you should make. He will lead you. He will guide you. At the right time, the *Scriptures say you will *reap a harvest of blessing if you don't give up. So don't give up, don't lose heart, and keep moving forward, with God by your side.

"That is why we never give up. Though our bodies are dying, our spirits are being renewed every day. For our present troubles are small and won't last very long. Yet they produce for us a glory that vastly outweighs them and will last forever! So we don't look at the troubles we can see now; rather, we fix our gaze on things that cannot be seen. For the things we see now will soon be gone, but the things we cannot see will last forever." 2 Corinthians 4:16-18 NLT

Questions

What can you do to ensure you do the right thing?

In what ways does Jesus lead you in your life?

Date:

Key words:

My Thoughts

Pray about everything

Don't worry about anything; instead, pray about everything.
Tell God what you need, and thank Him for all He has done.
Philippians 4:6 NLT

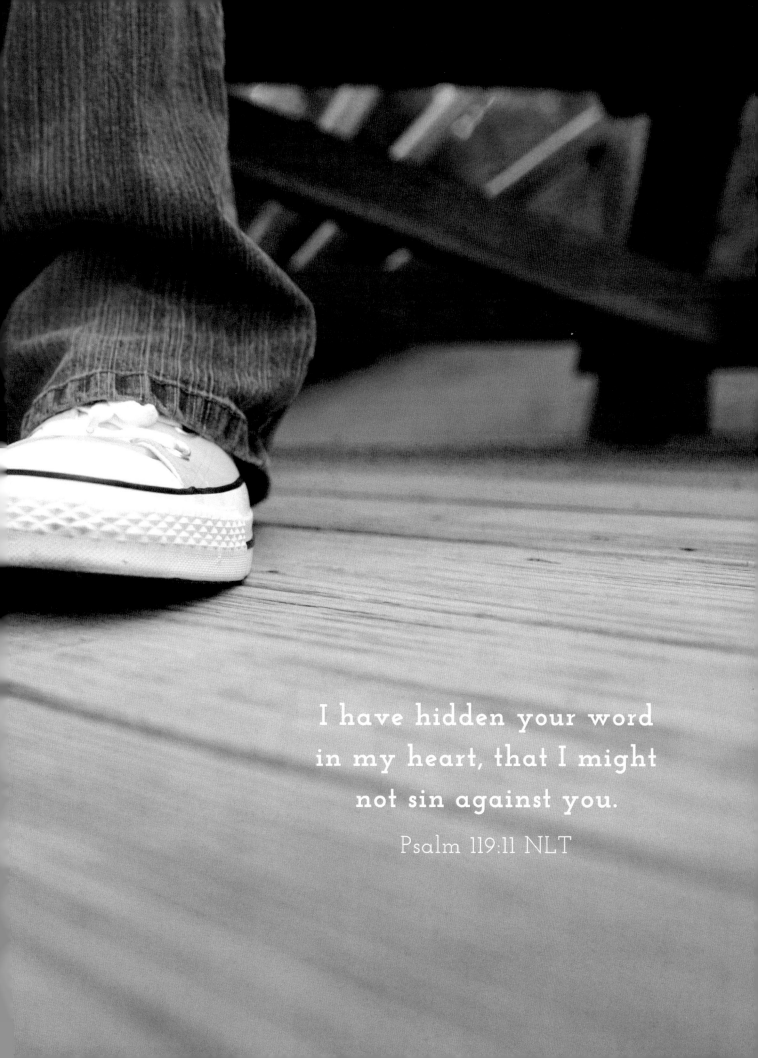

I have hidden your word
in my heart, that I might
not sin against you.

Psalm 119:11 NLT

Dictionary

A well when filled will never run dry: The Holy Spirit whom Jesus gave to us as a gift the moment we believed, courses through us like a river. The Holy Spirit, that Jesus gives, will flow through you and will create in you a well to draw from. In good times and in bad. If you continue to draw from God's Word through the Holy Spirit your well will not dry up. It will spring forth your faith in Him, it will spring forth your hope in Him. It will spring forth your eternal life in Him. John 7:37-39 NIV *"On the last and greatest day of the festival, Jesus stood and said in a loud voice, "Let anyone who is thirsty come to me and drink. Whoever believes in me, as Scripture has said, rivers of living water will flow from within them." By this he meant the Spirit, whom those who believed in him were later to receive. Up to that time the Spirit had not been given, since Jesus had not yet been glorified."*

Blessed: Favored by God

Calling: Your calling is what God has placed on your life to do. What He has created you to be.

Character: Helps define who a person is. Do they have good morals, any values? Are they honest and have integrity?

Compassion: Occurs when you see or hear of someone hurting and are compelled to make the person feel better within the situation. You might even take this a step further and try to better their situation. Love in action.

Confidence: To stand firm in what you believe. Belief in yourself to do what is right.

Corrupt: Someone who is dishonest and will do whatever they feel is necessary to get what they want. Morally void in the thoughts and actions.

Discernment: Being able to look at and examine a situation from multiple angles to determine and understand it. To try and figure out what God's desire is within the situation.

Expectancy: Knowing that God can provide what you are asking for.

Faith: Is trust in who God says He is and the promises He has made. *"Now faith is confidence in what we hope for and assurance about what we do not see."* Hebrews 11:1

Forgiveness: Releasing the hurt and pain that someone has caused you. Allowing God to do a redeeming work in them. Removing yourself from the equation to leave room for God's justice to work. Trusting in God to deal with the other person in His way and His timing. Not forgetting what happened, but not allowing yourself to dwell on what happened, but all the while remembering the lessons learned through what occurred.

Grace: Unmerited or undeserving favor - getting what we don't deserve - God's intervention

Holy Spirit: The Holy Spirit is a gift given to you the moment you believe. The moment you place your trust in God. Jesus left you with an advocate, someone to help guide you. The Holy Spirit lives within you, guides you, and prompts you to do the right thing.

Honor: To hold someone in high esteem. To have and to show respect for the person because of their position. Even if their actions are not worthy of honor.

Intentionally: Doing something on purpose

Jesus follower: One who believes that Jesus died on the cross for our sins and rose from the dead and is alive today.

Kindness: Is looking towards the good of others expecting nothing in return. Selfless, outward seeking instead of inward-looking. Full of grace, mercy, and love.

Lead you to the cross: Teach you about the Bible. About who Jesus is, and God's promises to you. To take you to where Jesus made His ultimate sacrifice for you and me, to have reverence for Christ. To learn about Jesus.

Made on purpose for a purpose: You were not an accident. You were created by God, formed by His hands with intention. Put on this earth at just this time to do what God created you to do.

Meditate: Filling your mind with God's Word.

Mercy: Loving kindness, withholding of punishment - not getting what we deserve.

Obey: To listen closely and then comply with a directive given without mumbling or grumbling along the way.

Pray: Praying is communication with the Lord. Prayer is not only asking God for things but praising Him for what He has done. For what He will do, and what He chooses to do. Prayer should encompass a time of listening, taking the time to wait on the Lord to respond.

Pray without ceasing: Constant, non-stop. Praying is communication with the Lord. Please know that you can communicate with the Lord through your actions. What you do, how you act, how you respond, and what you say.

Reap a harvest of blessing: If you do right in this world, if you take care of others, if you speak truth and kindness, if you follow after Jesus, God will reward you with blessings, eternal life, instead of consequences for your actions or lack thereof.

Refined by Fire: A process to remove any impurities from your life. Being made clean.

Rejoice: Regardless of the situation, you can still have pure joy, because you trust in God and His promises in your life.

Repent: To turn completely away from.

Restore: To repair something that was broken, in this context a relationship.

Reverence: Deep respect for God.

Temptation: A desire to do something that you know is wrong.

To write on the tablet of your heart: To tuck away God's Word in your heart and to remember and draw from when needed.

Weep: To cry with intensity.

Wisdom: Starts with knowing God and trusting in Him. Wisdom is not an inward-facing focus, or selfish. With Godly wisdom, it places your focus on Him. It is not self-seeking, but instead, it is gentle and kind. Loving and pure. Full of mercy and doing good. Recognizing that Biblical values should be first and foremost in your life.

Workmanship: God created you. With His hands, he formed you. He molded you into who you are. Each hair on your head counted. Each day is written in His book before you came to be. You are known, and you are loved. You are valued.

Worship: An outward expression of who God is. We can express worship in many ways, and worship can take on many forms.

CREDIT TO:

Photographs and templates used with permission from the following, via Canva:

How to use page Photograph---Halfpoint
Table of contents page Photograph 1, Page 89---Photography by Syda Productions.
Table of contents Photograph 2, Page 35---Photography by Chatkaren studio.
Table of contents Photograph 3, Page 51---Photography by Florian Doppler.
Table of contents Photograph 4, Page 7---Photography by Uatp2.
Page 1---Photography by Vadmary.
Page 2---Template by Andrew Pixel.
Page 3---Photography by Ikostudio.
Page 3,9---Background Images by DAPA Images.
Page 4---Photography by JSBB123.
Page 5-6---Photography by Alena Leskova.
Page 8---Template by Janna Hagan.
Page 9---Photography by Snapwire.
Page 10---Photography by DusanManic.
Page 11-12---Photography by Belchonock.
Page 13---Photography by Elena Photo.
Page 14---Template by Stories No Worries.
Page 15---Photography by Valerii Honcharuk. Background Image by Antpkr.
Page 16---Photography by Darrya.
Page 17-18---Photography by Shamia Casiano.
Page 19-20---Photography by Pexels--2286921.
Page 21, 43, 65, 87---Photography by Floral Deco.
Page 23---Photography by Ekaterina_Marory.
Page 24---Background Image by Gstudioimagen2.
Page 25---Photography by Alessia Campoli. Background Image by BravissimoS.
Page 26---Photography by Chompoosuppa.
Page 27-28---Photography by NelliSyr.
Page 29---Photography by Tatyana Maximova.
Page 5, 11, 17, 27, 33, 30, 36, 39, 46, 49, 52, 55, 61, 68, 71, 77, 80, 83, 90, 93, 99, 102, 105---Template by Marketplace Designers.
Page 31---Photography by Comstock. Background Image by Chaloemphan.
Page 32---Photography by Nikitabuida.
Page 33-34---Photography by Christopher Bernard.
Page 37---Photography 1 by Simon Lehmann. Photography 2 by Kanzefar.
Page 38---Photography by Pexels-Photo-192467.
Page 39-40---Photogrpahy by Milan2099.
Page 41-42---Photography by Aradaphotography.
Page 45---Photography by The Rabbit Hole Pictures.
Page 47---Photography by SrdjanPav.

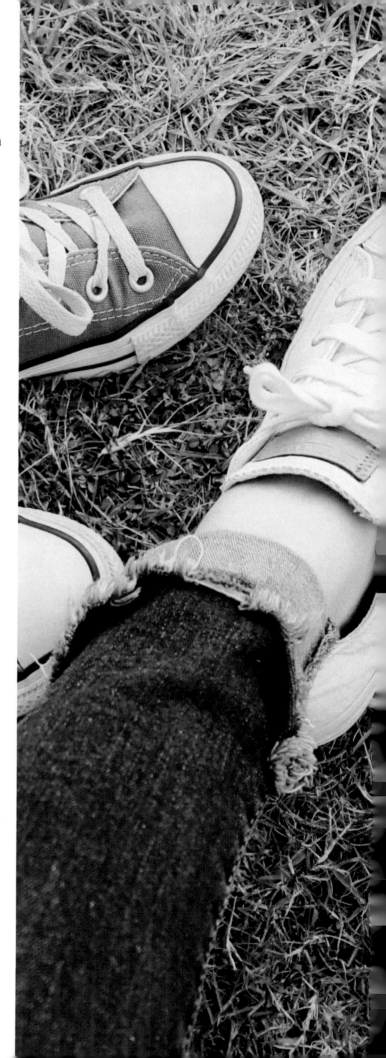

About the Author

Michele Arnold, wife, mother of 2, and Mmma (Grandma) to 1 (for now). In the midst of doting on her grandbaby, Michele runs a small business with her husband. Michele has written, taught, and facilitated Bible studies, one-day workshops, and simulcasts. She maintains and runs In His Grace Ministries webpage where you can find articles about faith, family, devotionals and so much more. Michele is passionate about family, leading, equipping and confirming women about who they are in Christ, following the Lord and His leading in her life and that of her family.

More from Michele Arnold

All throughout this devotional are ways to pray over, and for, your husband. We will delve into what it looks like being a wife and a woman of God and gain a better understanding of who we are in Christ. Let's consider some new thinking, based on timeless Biblical principles, contrasted against our current cultural and social norms. We have the life changing opportunity to gain a better understanding of how to move through your marriage and life in general, through God's lens. We have all gone through moments of great joys and deep pains. I pray that the words on these pages fill you with hope, peace, and a sense of who God is, and also, a sense of who you are in Christ.

I am's are a positive affirmation of who your daughter is in Christ. A gentle reminder of her importance to Christ and the world. When we speak over our children about who they are in Christ they become equipped to handle what the world throws at them. The I am's give your daughters the confidence needed to pursue their calling and help them to know their true identity in Christ.

I am's are a positive affirmation of who your son is in Christ. A gentle reminder of his importance to Christ and the world. When we speak over our children about who they are in Christ they become equipped to handle what the world throws at them. The I am's give your sons the confidence needed to pursue their calling and help them to know their true identity in Christ.

Hope is a word we use too often to express a desire for that which may occur but definitely is not certain. However hope in Christ is a different kind of hope. It is a hope that can be banked on, trusted, and waited for with anticipation that is rooted in promises made and met. There is truly no more uplifting feeling than placing your trust in a hope that can be relied on. When we plant ourselves in God's hope, we can trust He is faithful to finish the good work started in us.

Peace is a word we seem to use far and few between, but with God we can experience His peace every day. Even when our circumstances don't seem to align with peaceful feelings, you can be at peace in heart, soul, and mind. There truly is no greater feeling than being in complete peace. When we choose this peace, as God's free gift, we are set free and we are free indeed.

Made in the USA
Monee, IL
19 February 2021